RAMMAR
BASICS

ADVERBS
KATE RIGGS

CREATIVE C EDUCATION

Published by Creative Education P.O. Box 227, Mankato, Minnesota 56002
Creative Education is an imprint of The Creative Company www.thecreativecompany.us

Design and production by Liddy Walseth Art direction by Rita Marshall
Printed in the United States of America

Photographs by Corbis (Fritz Hoffmann/In Pictures), Getty Images (Michael Blann, Dave King,
National Geographic, Hitoshi Nishimura, Joel Sartore, Kim Sayer, Gandee Vasan),
iStockphoto (Emmanuel Hidalgo, Eric Isselée, Kevin Klöpper, Sean Locke,
Arpad Nagy-Bagoly, james steidl, syagci)

Library of Congress Cataloging-in-Publication Data
Riggs, Kate.
Adverbs / by Kate Riggs.
p. cm. — (Grammar basics)
Summary: A simple overview of adverbs—the words that describe actions—including their uses in
sentences, their degrees of comparison, and how to spot different and irregular forms.
Includes index.
ISBN 978-1-60818-237-4
1. English language—Adverb—Juvenile literature. 2. English
language—Grammar—Juvenile literature. I. Title.
PE1325.R54 2012
428.2—dc2 2011050851

First Edition
2 4 6 8 9 7 5 3 1

TABLE OF CONTENTS

INTRODUCTION

Do you get to school *quickly*? Do you eat out *often*? Is your favorite place *downstairs* in the basement? Do you *ever* play video games?

WHAT ARE ADVERBS?

The cat walked *quietly* behind the mouse.

Adverbs are words that show *how*, *when*, *where*, *how much*, or *why* things happen. Most adverbs are words that end in *–ly*. Here are some *–ly* adverbs you may know: *certainly, fearfully, horribly, only*. But not all words that end in *–ly* are adverbs.

ADVERBS IN USE

The pets waited *patiently* for their food.

Adverbs are used with **verbs**, **adjectives**, or other adverbs. They are never used with **nouns**. Adverbs can be anywhere in a **sentence**. Sometimes they are right before or after a verb.

DEGREES
OF ADVERBS

A bird flies
more quickly
than it walks.

Most adverbs have three degrees, or levels. The first level of an adverb tells something about a verb without likening it to anything else. The second level of an adverb compares two things. The third level of an adverb compares at least three things.

ADVERBS
THAT COMPARE

An adverb that compares two things often ends in *-er*. If you are talking about a car, you might say:

A car goes *fast*. It can go *faster* than other cars.

Sometimes the words *more* or *less* are used to compare adverbs:

Sarah talked *more* quietly than other girls.

THE HIGHEST
LEVELS

It is *best* to
have many
friends.

Adverbs of the third level explain what we do *best* or *worst*, too. These adverbs usually end in *–est* or use the words *most* or *least*. But look at the two adverbs in the first sentence on this page: *Best* is the third level of *well*. *Worst* is the third level of *badly*.

IRREGULAR FORMS

The small dog was a *little* afraid of the big dog.

Why are *best/well* and *worst/ badly* spelled so differently? Adverbs that have such different forms in each level are called irregular. Another irregular adverb is *little*. Can you find the other levels of *little* in the sentences below?

Anna ate less than Steve. Scott ate the least.

ALWAYS AND FOREVER

Chicks *always*
hatch from eggs to
become big birds.

Certain adverbs do not have any levels at all. They cannot be compared. *Always* cannot become *always-er* or *always-est*. And *now* cannot be *more now* or *most now*. These adverbs *always* stay the same!

LOOK OUT FOR
ADVERBS!

Adverbs tell us more about *how* and *when* actions take place. They help give meaning to the verbs in our lives. We could live without them. But we would not live *happily ever after*!

GRAMMAR GAME TIME

Have you ever done a Mad Lib? This is a story that lets you fill in the blanks with your own words. Use what you know about adverbs to do the Mad Lib on the next page. Be sure to write your adverb choices on another sheet of paper!

On a planet _____ (adverb: *where*) away lived an alien. He was the _____ (adverb: *how much*) alien left in his city. One day, the alien ran _____ (adverb: *how*) to the next city. He ran so _____ (adverb: *how*) that he tripped! _____ (adverb: *when*) he felt even _____ (irregular adverb: *how*). _____ (adverb: *when*) he saw his friend! His friend said, "I thought you were _____ (adverb: *when*) going to get here!"

grammar word bank

adjectives—words that explain *what kind*, *how many*, and *which*
nouns—words that name people, places, and things
sentence—a group of words that has a noun as the subject and a verb
verbs—action or state of being words; state of being words include *am*, *is*, *are*, *was*, and *were*

read more

Fleming, Maria. *Grammar Tales: Tillie's Tuba*. New York: Scholastic, 2004.

Heller, Ruth. *Up, Up and Away: A Book about Adverbs*. New York: Grosset & Dunlap, 1991.

web sites

Grammar Blast
http://www.eduplace.com/kids/hme/k_5/grammar/
Test your adverb knowledge by taking the quiz at your grade level.

Grammar Ninja
http://www.kwarp.com/portfolio/grammarninja.html
Skilled ninjas can find the adverbs, nouns, and verbs in each sentence.

index